for Tom
all the Best!
Duane
June, 1990

Songs for the Harvester of Dreams

Poems by Duane Niatum

University of Washington Press

Seattle & London

Copyright © 1981 by Duane Niatum
Printed in the United States of America
By The Haddon Craftsmen
Avanta Type with Dwiggens Electra Florets
Book Design by Audrey Meyer

Library of Congress Cataloging in Publication Data

Niatum, Duane, 1938–
    Songs for the harvester of dreams.

    1. Indians of North America—Poetry.   I.   Title.
PS3564.I17S65   811'.54   80–50864
ISBN 0–295–95758–1

*For Marc, my son,
and the Children
of the First Americans*

✎ Acknowledgments

The following poems have been published previously. The author and publisher gratefully acknowledge permission to reprint.

American Poetry Review: "Eagle."
Argus (Seattle): "Question of the Forest."
Beloit Poetry Journal: "Sky of Departing."
Chariton Review: "The Art of Clay."
Combinations: "Seattle Memoir."
Contact II: "Woman of the Moon."
Dacotah Territory: "Death's Song" and "Raven Dancer."
El Nahuatzen: "Song of Origin."
Nation: "Paddle Song," "Klallam Song," and "Crow's Catastrophe."
Niagara: "A Terrapin Joy."
Northwest Indian News: "Loon" and "Grasshopper."
Northwest Review: "Light Moments in February."
Pacific: "Good Omen."
Pacific Search: "Whale Song," "Wolf," "Kingfisher," "Spider," "Owl," "Summer," "Squirrel," and "The Bear."
Phoebe: "The Words" and "Loon."
Poetry Now: "Timebird."
Puget Soundings: "Cougar" "The Chant of Sore Eye Moon," and "The Little Disturbances This March."
Seattle Review: "To the Fisherman, Salmon, the Northwest Waters" and "First Spring."
Seattle Times: "Trickster's Hour."
Twigs: "All We Need."
University of Tampa Review: "Heron at Low Tide" and "The Seed."
"The Canoe" first appeared as a broadside from Strawberry Press, New York (copyright © 1977 by Duane Niatum).

Many of the shorter poems were previously published as a chapbook, *Turning to the Rhythms of Her Song,* Jawbone Press, Seattle (copyright © 1977 by Duane Niatum). Some poems in this volume have been revised.

Contents

Part I. Voices from the World and Its People

Part II. Spinning the Dream Wheel

PART I

❧ *Voices from the World and Its People*

Dream of the Burning Longhouse

Spinning away from the center,
Lost to the flames,
The old ones break down to shadow and ash.
Am I banished from the country of my blood?
Has my heart thrown the drum to the earth?
My spirit lost its song to the river?
Oh my body, have we reached your water cave?

Spring

It is late in awakening you,
But its orange slope changes your direction.

You hear a door slam shut,
See the last woman lock the room you swear

Was never yellow as this pine.
Outside, moving as the sun moves, you try

Burying the new failure under the last
Mound of your bones. You see it's

Not a question of travel,
But seeing your scars are not strange.

❧ Paddle Song

Tangled in a net off our village shore,
Seals emerge from somewhere we have never been.
Bobbing like corks beside our canoe,
What could such sea-deepened eyes
Be telling us, of what storm, what loss,
We failed to name on thundering fool's day?

Question of the Forest

Arrow, cedar, mask, and star,
What keeper strikes the drum:
The river calling tyee salmon,
Or, the woman of white pine
Picking berries well into dusk?

Death's Song

Their bones rattle home
To my heartless mound alone;
I who shatter the sun,
Chant for no one.

Summer

Call it the reason we praise
Each color we find in a name;
Call it the reason we see
Only Trickster and ourselves
Turn pain into song,
The yellow bird into stone.

The Seed

It opens in the dawn branches,
Closes when you're half-asleep.
Tomorrow it might build a nest
In the tiny hand of a child,
Or under grandmother's stick
Digging roots in blackbird's field.

🍂 *Klallam Song*

What creature lights the deep pools of your eyes,
Within the circle of your dreaming,
O woman who sleeps in my heart?
Because I am poor, a maker of song,
I fly slowly round the luminous branches
Of your moontree, offer you this fire,
O woman who sleeps in my heart.

Woman of the Moon

Grandmother says
She can't be seen with the eye,
But the dream.
Dances in your shadow when you
Offer her beads shaped by the seasons.
She will find the colors of your heart
If she desires to balance
Your vision with her own,
Your nerves with her embrace,
Her body naked in your arms.

❧ *The Bear*

When it is the river's net,
We watch for the stroke
To draw light from the salmon.

When it is the river's net,
We are the spirits of the rapids,
Eat these words for the salt.

Raven Dancer

He rises from the hemlock side of the moon—
Starts the fire for the people,
To warm the lost, the weary, the homeless.
When his eyes find you, the fan of daybreak
Will shape the ashes, your soul clapping
In the light of anonymity.

Wolf

The shy friend that guards your path.
In the wind of seven mornings,
He calls you from the village
With his white-throated song.
Wait quietly, his winter count will take
You back to the first world of snow.

Grasshopper

Riding the wind on a large orange leaf,
It swirls through the colors
At the end of dry grass moon;
Dreams of migrating geese
Honking across the yellow sky,
Its body awakening to the first chill
Rising like the river.

Loon

FOR SARAH NEARN

It grows lighter in the water
Like a ripple from the black star,

The moon turning the lake to copper.
Is it the carrier of summer's final thread?

Easing effortlessly into evening's darkness,
It dives for the lower reaches of your eyes.

At its place for dreaming, it builds a nest
With twigs made from escaping stars.

Kingfisher

Those speckled trout leaping the rapids,
With tails collecting more light than Rainbow—
Those dragonflies claiming new shadow,
With wings reaching more stars than mole—
Have I caught the spirits that bring the dawn,
And if so, how will I see them asleep?

✒ *The Words*

We are not sad to see them give their legends
Back to the sea. The loss is joyous,
The way winter builds a home in our heart.
Even when memory has dragged us to its cave,
Loosened the earth under our feet
With new defeats, deaths, and loves,
They comfort our village with a lost totem—
Carve a path out of the dream to crab's retreat
Where we kiss like two fish separating the moon.

Good Omen

In the woods, at the longhouse site
Of Old Patsy, my great-great-grandfather,
My love hears a green voice drift
Among the willows along the path,
His one-hundred-twenty-eight-year life.
She carries a feather found on the beach
To honor his chant to salmon and osprey.
Circling her silence with his own,
A goldfinch trades her paths,
One shrill note pausing in the surfgrass.

The Canoe

Fungus buried, mossy as Elwah River mist,
It is the remains of Old Man's totem.
On this earth you must breathe like the evergreens
Where this elder carved lean animals
Of the sun on his paddles, or Seatco
Will beat you songless,
Blind you to what these shadows yield.

Whale Song

I call to it roaming beneath fog's wing,
Paddle toward deeper waters to find myself,
Be shade for every creature moving or still,
Dream when it follows the storm down the night,
So I may again see the village fires,
Wild with a trail of dancers.

ஃ Klallams from the Village of White Fir

FOR MY SON, MARC

Child
A darting splash of strawberries
Soul of the earth
Lopes like elk into the camas field—
Tosses summer to mallard and crow,
A cedar child running for the sun.

Old Cedar
A mind of many fish
Eye of the forest
Sits dreaming of the ancestor
Who turns the moon into a moth
That dances forever in the dark.

Cougar

His solitude warms our blood
As he runs from our eyes
Following him into the brush.
What strength we have left
In our hearts goes back to him.

Squirrel

O dip your hands into these crimson leaves,
Build your nest with this wind,
Give the storm a way to your heart.
Then one morning when you step softly
Through my soul's shy forest,
The snow will name your footprints,
Keep your promises open to the cold.

Heron at Low Tide

No wonder Young Patsy
Saw him as the sun's firstborn.
He stands in shallow water,
So like the wind's reed
That I almost feel his break
From this world snap
Once for my memory.

Eagle

The force he gathers at his wingtips from the rains
Cascades down the full length of your spine,
Spreads through your blood
That drags his talons to earth.
You later dream a bird
Rests on the blackest ledge,
Underneath your retina that feeds
Fear a greater hunger.
Until you dance with the animals you destroy,
His wing will never find your shadow.

Spider

Stop, friends, watch me spin past
The morning rain, the morning rain.
Touch the yellow, orange, and green threads—
Feel Thunder's colors pass through my house!

And if by chance, by accidental dance,
We meet where the meadow's a ledge of violets,
Don't be frightened of my drumming.

There are things about you, too beautiful to lose;
There are songs for you, not even Raven knows.

The Chant of Sore Eye Moon

FOR MARC

Don't laugh at me too soon;
I give the lost the moon.

I scatter the snowy creature
Burying itself in the pine

Like a blue jay, one
Wing to a shadow.

Don't look at me too long,
I blind all with my song.

I cover mother earth with a silence
The sleeping bears hear.

Don't wink when I'm not there;
I give the lost the moon.

28

Raven and the Fear of Growing White

When the legends cannot feed the village fire,
When mother spruce answers no child in the dark,
When hawk fails to reach his shadow on the river,
When First Woman beats hummingbird to the earth,
And salmon eats the rapids until his bones shatter,
When otter steals the long-awaited promises of stars,
And blue jay stops naming each new storm,
It will end its fear of growing white.

Owl

You will find my feather floating
On the next wave to beach this Sound;
It shall leave your mind at the blue window;
Give you the Duwamish River's way
Of offering it all to the sea,
Offering it all to the sea.

PART II

Spinning the Dream Wheel

Cedar Man

I

He grows calmer at the beach,
As he waits for the wood
To talk to his hands,
Now barren of fury
Three seasons.

Drifting with the bones, shells,
And agate at his feet,
The dark calling him to dig
For his life, he whittles
Out confusion.

II

He kneels to cup the water
To his lips, salt his spirit
With the way fools dance in fog.
He feels the currents that swirl
In an octopus's eye.

He remembers the woman at home,
The healing poise of her body.
Do the birds flying all directions
Know if he'll hold her the way
Light holds cedar?

III

He cannot be weary of the wind
If the weaver is the voice of old friends.
He follows each wave of the sky
Falling to the last cliff, the last rock,
The last shadow.

Called by the creature he
Sees as formless haze, he offers
It more space by starting a fire
While the night fossils the star tracks
Of his nerves.

Seattle Memoir

It is the twist
In the sky,
The night wind.

It mirrors not only
You and the nomad's
Dog of despair,

But the sea,
Its rocket windows,
Masks of sand,

Foam, and tides.
A woman, shy, marries
Her soul to the dark,

Her amber eyes
Caves of suicide,
Failure, pages as empty

As the bridge.
Tumbling over,
Her arms embrace

The void. The lean
Man of summer
Cannot believe her eyes

Said, *Go away,*
Leave me be.
Swallows drift off

With the secret
The stars gave to
His dream anchor,

The woman who leaped
Into herself.

All We Need

I

To skip pebbles
Across the architecture of the pond;
To plunge ourselves
Into its
Sky.

To hear swallows
Dip eastward toward their master,
The insects
Hunger.

To fall in
The grass, fern, pine needles, and cones;
The forest
Interflow.

II

To keep earth,
Shade, and wings by our side;
Awaken to
The crickets' motion,
A hummed fusion
For Eros.

To be buoyant
As water lilies, weave our bodies into August;
Mime dragonfly
And star.

And in exhaustion,
Cheer the sudden rains, the speech of lightning,
Before the evening lets us
Go.

Light Moments in February

I

Bridge patterns
Turn on the morning.
Sunlight pours through beams—
The mill's solitude.

II

Crocus,
Orange with awakening,
Earth's keeper of yet another plane
Of color.

III

Geese
Arguing in circles.
The pond is a seizure
Of white cacophony!

IV

Still,
The rain never answers.
So the mallards
Move to the edge of the moment,
Somewhat uneasy because the center
Is missing.

V

What is it
The wind has abandoned?
Us or its own loss of gravity?

VI

The suppleness
Of the willow. If only our pride
Could leave memory,
Wind's dancer!

VII

Midnight,
Austere messenger of the shadows.
What thief or lover is blind to starlight?

The Art of Clay

The years in the blood keep us naked to the bone.
So many hours of darkness we fail to sublimate.
Light breaks down the days to printless stone.

I sing what I sang before, it's the dream alone.
We fall like the sun when the moon's our fate.
The years in the blood keep us naked to the bone.

I wouldn't reach your hand, if I feared the dark alone;
My heart's a river, but is not chilled with hate.
Light breaks down the days to printless stone.

We dance for memory because it's here on loan.
And as the music stops, nothing's lost but the date.
The years in the blood keep us naked to the bone.

How round the sky, how the planets drink the unknown.
I gently touch; your eyes show it isn't late.
Light breaks down the days to printless stone.

What figures in this clay? Gives a sharper hone?
What turns the spirit white? Wanting to abbreviate?
The years in the blood keep us naked to the bone.
Light breaks down the days to printless stone.

Walking in an Evening of Crackling Branches

The wind says
It is the same wall
In New York, Topeka, or Seattle:
Frost calling you to come out;
Enjoy the light.

This January promises
A dark street, night, the ashes of stars.
In the cedars, the cold slides apart
Always in your path.
Your body's woodsman.

Thinking oblivion caught
You in its net, you
Run up the street incognito.
The door opens like your nerves,
Whistling for blood.

You pretend grey
Colors the ruins with style,
Your hair with class.
Into the forties, you age
What time notes.

🝆 *The Little Disturbances This March*

The wind pushes me sideways,
Forward, then back,
While the street keeps adding distances.

At its old routine, the winter star
Spins the headless selves
Round and round and round,
Offers a shadow for the one
Who may reach home.

Unable to ignore what passes
For an afternoon, the eyes
I used to travel with rebel, join forces
With the feet in the last cave,
These unobtrusive shoes about to self-destruct.

So, out of respect for the remains,
No one cares who waves
The white flag first
At evening's final stop sign.

And when the hairy selves appeared,
We started the peace dance,
One, two, three!

❧ Journey to the Islands

Cows stumbling on to morning,
Their bells ringing in the maples,
Shapeless as the hill,
The cornfields spinning like fish,
The mountains reaching zero,
Tomorrow, the bell in the sand.

All is water to the eye:
The freeway, the bus,
The blood's light pulse,
The beach, shell mounds,
The sunweb on the sea.

Sky elders, the stars—
Since they chart the tides,
We carry the moon-net,
Its stone faces of kelp,
Our devils gambling failure.

The fragile voices of exile:
Ourselves remembering evening losses,
The air between
Feather and storm,
Gravity's compass, the balance hoop.

Clouds paler than snapshots,
Seasonal whirlwinds:
Snipes arguing in refuse,
Waves in tufts of color,
And memory, the island echoes,
What tumbles us in sleep.

Timebird

It is the last to say good-by
        To the lovers,

The thief, the old. Getting lost
        In the visible,

It shapes itself past the dogwood,
        Leaving the river

Again without memory. Deep inside
        Tomorrow's cave,

Hermit voices exit to greet the creature
        Their solitude requires.

They learned long ago to promise owl,
        Who touches them,

Anything, for it is he who buries his toes
        In mud for the faithless.

Imaginary Drawings of Song Animals

I

Treefrog winks
Without springing from its elderberry hideaway.
Before the day is buried in dusk,
I will trust the crumbling earth.

II

Foghorns, the bleached absence
Of the Cascade Mountains, Olympics.
The bay sleeps in a bell of haze.
Anchorless as the night,
The blue-winged teal dredges for moonlight.

III

Thistle plumed,
A raccoon pillages my garbage.
What have we done to memory?
Whose footprints abandon the stone?

IV

Dams abridge the Columbia Basin.
On the rim of a rotting fish barrel,
A crow. The imperishable
Remains of cedar man's shield.

V

Shells, gravel musings from the deep,
Dwellings from the labyrinth of worms.
Crabs crawl sideways into another layer of dark.

VI

Deer
Dwellings the freeway—
Don't graze near us, don't run in our words.
We hold your ears in our teeth.

VII

Bumblebee,
A husk of winter and the wind.
I will dance in your field
If the void is in bloom.

VIII

A lizard appears, startled by the basket
Of blackberries. In the white
Of the afternoon we are lost to the stream.
Forty years to unmask the soul!

Sky of Departing

Bone whistle:
At the river, hoofbeats
Of horses on the ice,
White crystals nameless in song.

A feather drifts in the snow.
I think of spring, granite
Veins beneath Montana plains,
Amplifying the belly of the sun.

Orange-striped bug of the aspen,
Trampling the bookstore counter,
Where else will you outwit the storm?

Beyond windows, all paths
Merge where the mind
Is a stone among stars.

Surfacing through clouds, the jet,
Its winter trail following
The ancestors, following buffalo.

Twirling on its flame
Of earth and sky, the moon
Dangles from a ring.

Home, in our mountains, I sweat
For what the spirit counts.

æ *The Green Window*

I

Next door, a woman
Rests her face
On the window ledge.

What reunion touches her
Shoulder with the light
Of the afternoon?

Her eyes narrow to
A robin perched on
A blue television antenna.

All these currents cross
The distances in suspension,
Walls hollow as leaves.

II

In the garden beyond
A man counts roses
Breaking into bud near

His moss doorstone.
Has he always been
Framed in her refractions?

What woman has returned
To arrange the roses
In his shaking hands?

With her vertigo brush,
She clips its foliage,
Tiny promises.

Song of Origin

The dream animals break
Us down to names.
The smog spills its image
Into the invisible veins

Of the hill, and the sun
Asleep in its cage.
The yellow rose hangs over water,
The stones claiming dust,

The dust, our bones
Elemental to the roots.

A Terrapin Joy

It is when you run faster
And faster through the loop
The wind hollows to sand;
It is when you toss a shell
To hear what lights forever;

It is to skip and not laugh
When sandpiper says, with a foot
On the distance, *Shake loose*
This echo, and we'll fold
Hello wings, back to back!

❧ The Musician

You often played
On sheets of dawn,
Your notes building
A room in our house.
Your visits were brief
Retrievals lost to dusk,
Our coming of age,
Time's eraser.

We miss you most
When the snow falls
And hardens to crystal,
When the attic mice
Sleep in the candlelight
We burn on stairways
And in the room
They nest in all winter.

You're the secret sharer.
What moon went bronze,
What measure surrendered
The colors of the peonies
At the concerto's end?
Your sound, a sapphire fountain,
Transparent as the river.
What warmth of place

In our hearts explodes
With your absence. Oh
Why did you leave
The piano, the city
Unannounced? What melody drove
You from our lives?

We feel marginal. Yet,
The lines on our faces

Keep returning the hours
You composed the silence.
In our imperfections
And the pizzicato refrains
Of adventurous leaves, we wait
For the piano to open
The window, our souls
To skip on water.

To the Fisherman, Salmon, the Northwest Waters

I have long forgotten
The last beach, its direction
To the wreckage you abandoned.
There is not even an anchor

Or rib to mark where you
Sailed your boat onto the rocks
Off the gyrating, whale-shoaled
San Juan Islands.

What wind composes this song?
What can I tell my son?
You were an illusion
I battled in storms
I once called home?

And what builds a nest
In the dream wheel
Is the green-throated dawn,
Its cloudbursting waves
That soak me to the marrow,

But without your deceptive history.
And only when I slip
On an inclined path crumbling
Before my eyes does your
Ghost chuckle it chipped

My shadow to salt for laughs.
Now eighteen winters grind
The tides, sand, fish into my joints,
The morning you sent all
The maimed birds to the sky.

How you mocked my fear
Like a beached walrus.
Do your indifferent eyes,
Rolling in and out of my darkness
Like the breakers, prove

Grandfather was right, when he
Said you were an idler, a liar,
Danceless and songless to the end?
Today I hurtle your name

Into the black seas: to break
Your hide-and-seek rejections,
End my search for you
Who could not call me—son.

Crow's Catastrophe

The wind whips once, twice, three
Times around its body,
Its toes wired to the cold.
Cracking like the leaves,
It squawks at the rain claws

Tearing out its feathers.
Inside, we almost feel guilty
We're not this livid clown,
The storm's caw-eyed little brother,
Frozen to another joke.

Album of the Labyrinth of Doors

I

She left me a room for the wounds.
Since two seasons turned gray,
I feel it must be her gift.

II

When a downcast face rises with a smile,
Greets you among the market strangers,
Your feet of clay loosen
From the weight of your being.

III

The woman I saw climb the long stairs
To the tower of last night's dream.
Was she coming or going?
And was it me standing by the window
Waiting for what to change the room?
What we separate, or what separates us?

IV

I learn to keep the dream wheel nearby.
Its soul is more than likely mine.
If I lose, my spirit will be yours.

V

Do we burn down the doors with our lives
To meet the storm's center?
Could this be our song of despair?

VI

The animals that enter the nightmare
Do not leave me with fear, but myself.
What they never roar,
I hear on the nights when I am a verb of solitude.

VII

As his feet touch the street,
He knows he should have spoken to the woman
On the bus who offered him her isolation.
Is cruelty the failure
Of the voice to answer chance?

VIII

You go on writing these words
Because they go on leading you beyond themselves.
The truth lies between connections.

IX

Mostly, we chose to circle in regret.
What we lost was the circle, not regret.

X

We counted too much on pain,
Learned after it shuffled on with our scars,
That it was there in the body of joy.
Now we call silence the fugitive.

XI

Out of pity, he stands before the mirror;
He has a question for it;
Just as he is about to release the demons,
The mirror crumbles. Still,
Years later, he thinks it answered.

XII

When you begin counting the losses,
You are already lost.

XIII

I was glad to be born on Friday, the thirteenth,
In icy winds. From this hoop
I inherited my histories of ruin.

XIV

You bury in memory's shifting mud
The promises you never keep.
Otherwise, why the need for failure?

XV

I call autumn the Trickster;
It calls me the dream's myopic student.
Next summer, I will grow
More close to the small.

XVI

If I could choose one road in my life,
Death could keep its song.

XVII

My friends say I am a hermit.
The last two women who entered and left
My circle agreed with them.
When will they see the bird
Bouncing off their window is my heart
Returning to nest in their names?

XVIII

As a tribute to the apparitions we become,
Let's zig-zag our way down the city;
Sing to the void, to what humbles us.

૭૯ Trickster's Hour

Are you the one the storm
Has left to shoulder the rain
That hollows the wall?

Do you mind if pain
Makes a window of your presence?

Can your feet at the river's edge
Balance your shadow on the rocks,
The scar tribe on the jawbone of a crow?

Do you chill swiftly when the wind
Is the desert, the desert is your song?

Are your friends the words
You can't remember from their dance?

Have you watched a line escape,
Then return to the web on your face?

Is your body collapsing from the bones,
Now a flutist for the ants?

Has a monarch butterfly mistaken your hand
For a leaf of hope?

Are you wondering how long to run
On the wheel of my questions?

First Spring

Drifting on the wheel
Of a past looking like
A redskin American gothic,
Staring through forty-one years
Of rain-pelted windows, I bear
With modest grace, diminished nerves,
Narrowing light, half-formed figures:
The memories floating in purgatory.

Renting a small house,
The first in fifteen years, I
Admire each hour the diffidence
Of the elders walking by,
Their eyes of snow-caves,
Their hands dancing like puppets.
When a lost love calls,
Having abandoned another,
I say, *Sorry, sorry, I'm*

Too busy with the friends
Still left. I'll call you.
The lie of copper on my tongue.
Why tell her they are
The birds at the feeder,
Bees in the lilacs and roses,
Books on the shelves,
Paintings on the walls,
Wind in the roof?

It is called giving your body
A field to get lost in.
It is called standing on your head
Before the women you lost.
It is called sleeping
In the embers of your name.

Duane Niatum was born in 1938 in Seattle, Washington. An American Indian, he is a member of the Klallam tribe, whose ancestral lands are on the Washington coast along the Strait of Juan de Fuca. His early life was spent in Washington, Oregon, California, and Alaska, and at age seventeen he enlisted in the Navy and spent two years in Japan. On his return he completed his undergraduate studies in English at the University of Washington. He later received his M.A. from The Johns Hopkins University. He is currently an American Indian Heritage consultant for the Seattle public schools.

Niatum's poetry has been published in the *Nation, Prairie Schooner, Northwest Review,* and many other literary journals and anthologies. His previously published collections of poems are *After the Death of an Elder Klallam, Ascending Red Cedar Moon,* and *Digging Out the Roots.* In 1973–74 he was the editor of the Native American Authors series at Harper and Row, and in 1975 he served as the editor of *Carriers of the Dream Wheel,* an anthology of Native American poetry.